TIME-TRAVEL GUIDES

The ANCIENT EGYPTIANS

SARAH RIDLEY

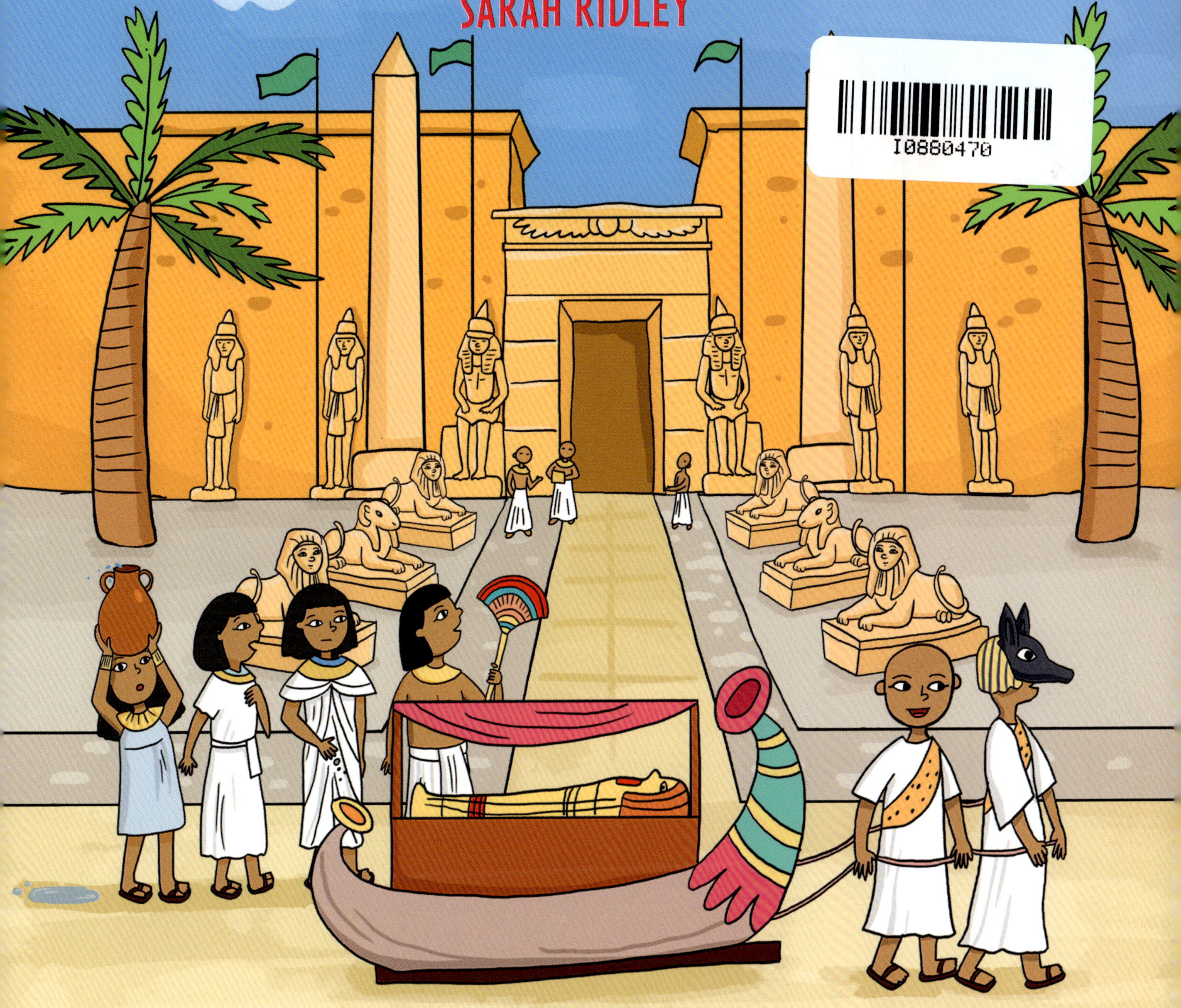

Gareth Stevens PUBLISHING

Please visit our website,
www.garethstevens.com.
For a free color catalog of all
our high-quality books, call
toll free 1-800-542-2595 or
fax 1-877-542-2596.

Cataloging-in-Publication Data

Names: Ridley, Sarah, 1963-, author.
Title: The Ancient Egyptians / Sarah Ridley.
Description: Buffalo, NY : Gareth Stevens Publishing, 2026. | Series: Time-travel guides | Includes glossary and index.
Identifiers: ISBN 9781482475395 (pbk.) | ISBN 9781482475401 (library bound) | ISBN 9781482475418 (ebook)
Subjects: LCSH: Egypt--Civilization--To 332 B.C.--Juvenile literature. | Egypt--Social life and customs--To 332 B.C.--Juvenile literature.
Classification: LCC DT83.R533 2026 | DDC 932--dc23

Published in 2026 by
Gareth Stevens Publishing
2544 Clinton St.
Buffalo, NY 14224

First published in Great Britain in 2022 by Hodder & Stoughton

Artwork and Design: Collaborate Agency
Editor: Sarah Silver

Picture credits:
p.4-5: © johnbraid/Shutterstock.com, p.28: © Vincenzo Iacovoni/Shutterstock.com,

Printed in China
CPSIA compliance information: Batch #QW26GS: For further information contact Gareth Stevens at 1-800-542-2595.

CONTENTS

THEBES

Welcome to Thebes, an important ancient Egyptian city. In the past, the Egyptians called their city Waset, but it is better known as Thebes, the name the ancient Greeks gave to the city. Just to confuse you further, today it's called Luxor.

Luxor is 310 miles (500 km) south of Cairo, the capital of modern Egypt. It's a popular place for tourists to visit, thanks to its amazing ancient Egyptian buildings. Historians and archaeologists have studied these buildings, as well as other ruins, objects, written records, and mummified bodies, to learn about the lives of the people who lived there thousands of years ago.

TIME-TRAVEL GUIDES

Your time-travel guide

Congratulations on buying this Time-Travel Guide, the must-have companion for travelers journeying into the past. The guide will give you advice on where to stay, what to wear, and how best to spend your time in Thebes. Top travel tips throughout will give you the low-down on what to bring, what to avoid, and what not to miss!

Top Tip

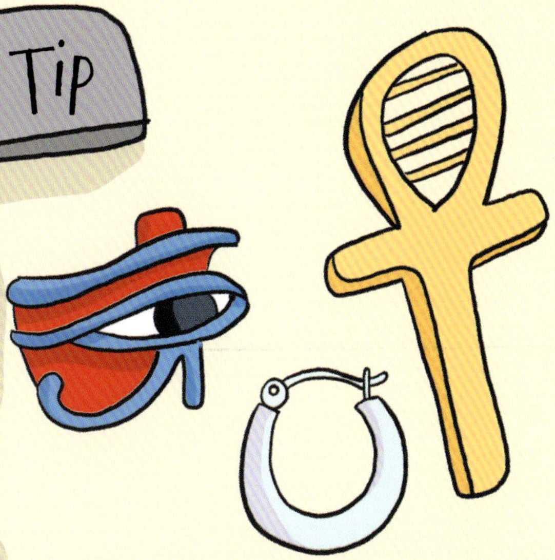

Bring some jewelry with you

The ancient Egyptians don't use coins to buy things. Instead, bring some small, beautiful objects, such as earrings, rings, and amulets made of gold or silver, or jewelry made of colorful pottery. You can swap these items for things you want in Thebes.

Time to go back

Now we will use time-travel technology to transport you back to visit Thebes about 3,300 years ago. Brace yourself: the ancient Egyptians lived very different lives than us!

PUTTING THEBES ON THE MAP

You are visiting Thebes during the time of Ramesses II (reigned 1279–1213 BCE), over 3,000 years ago. Ramesses II was a pharaoh, or king. By this time, many pharaohs have lived and died, ruling Egypt through a series of dynasties for almost 2,000 years. They have built up the power and wealth of the kingdom.

At this time, during the 19th Dynasty of Egypt, Per-Ramessu is Egypt's capital city, but Thebes is the center of ancient Egyptian religion. Use the map with page number references to help you find out more.

The kingdom of Egypt

Ramesses II rules over all ancient Egypt. However, at several times in the past, it was divided into Upper Egypt and Lower Egypt, with a king to rule each part. The River Nile flows north through the center of the country. In Lower Egypt, the river splits into channels to form the Nile Delta. Thebes is in Upper Egypt, where the weather is hot and dry for most of the year.

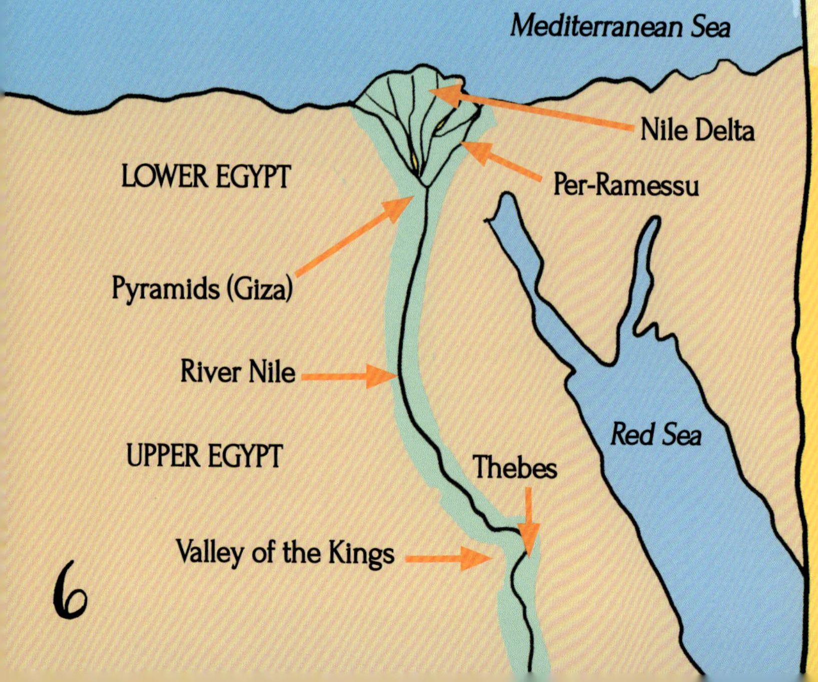

Thebes and the Nile

The city lies on the east bank of the River Nile. This is where most people live and work. There are two very important temples on this side of the river, both dedicated to the god Amun-Ra (see page 16), but you'll need to take a ferry to visit the Valley of the Kings and some other temples.

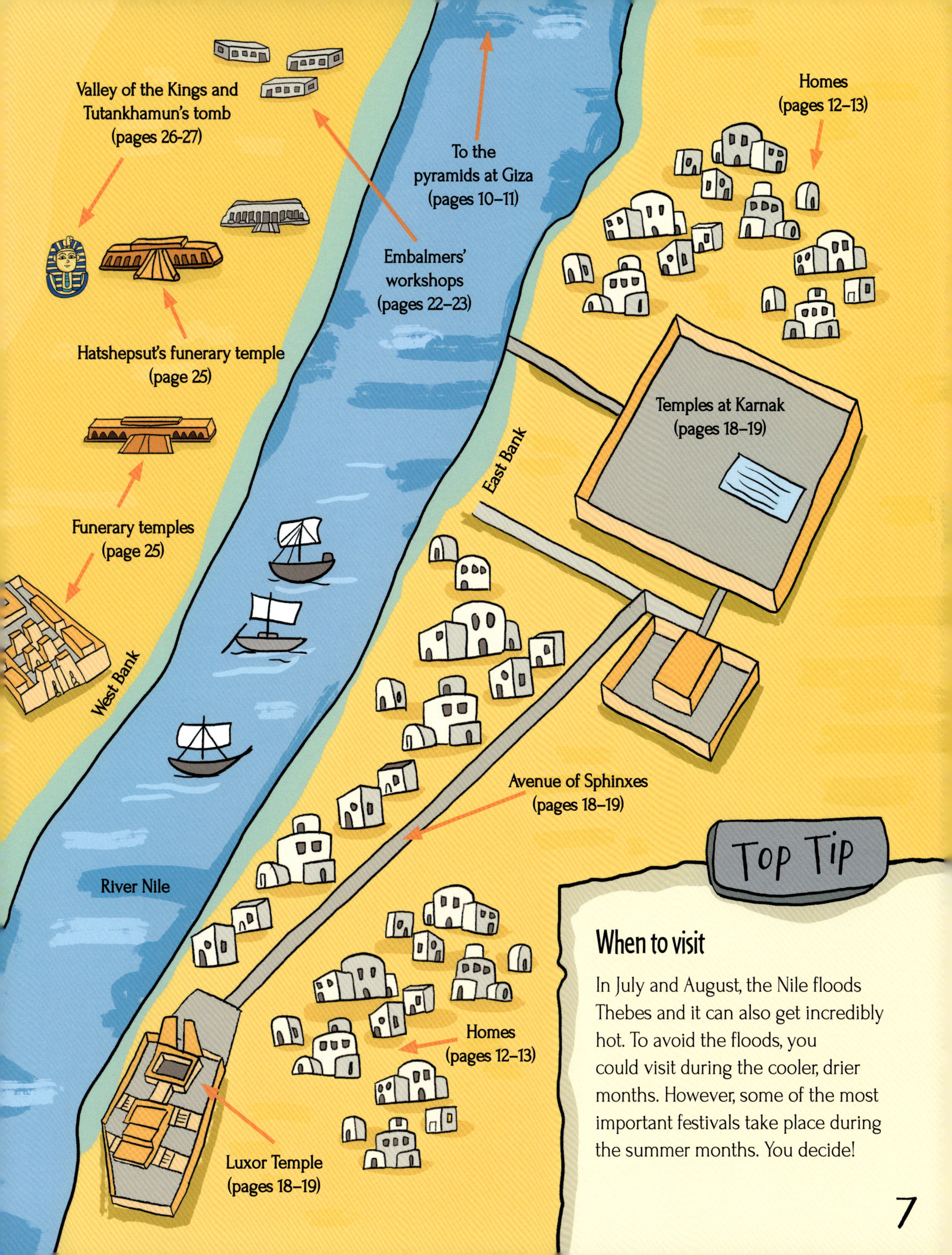

Top Tip

When to visit

In July and August, the Nile floods Thebes and it can also get incredibly hot. To avoid the floods, you could visit during the cooler, drier months. However, some of the most important festivals take place during the summer months. You decide!

SAIL UP THE NILE

The best way to get to Thebes is on a merchant ship along the River Nile. These ships are the main way to transport everything in ancient Egypt, including food, pottery, wine, huge stone building blocks, and people! From the boat you will spot people at work in fields. Most ancient Egyptians are farmers.

The gift of the Nile

Much of Egypt is desert. When the River Nile floods, it leaves land close to the river covered in a thick, rich layer of black mud that is good for crops. Farmers use plows pulled by hand or by ox to mix the mud into the land. Then the farmers plant seeds. They also trap and store floodwater for use during the growing season.

Farmers grow crops including wheat, barley, lentils, chickpeas, onions, leeks, and lettuces. In some places, farmers grow fruit trees and grape vines, as well as flax, which can be made into linen cloth.

Top Tip

Keep Hapi happy

Join the ancient Egyptians in keeping Hapi – the god of the Nile – happy by throwing gifts of food or objects into the river. Ancient Egyptians believe that Hapi has the power to bring the precious floods every year (see page 17).

Look out for: animals

People keep geese and ducks for their eggs and meat, and goats for milk. If they can afford it, a donkey or an ox helps them carry loads, plow fields, and work simple machines. Wealthy landowners have herds of cows, kept safe by herdsmen who bring them to the Nile to drink.

Using a shaduf

To move water from a canal or river to water crops in a field, farmers use a tool called a *shaduf*. They lower a bucket hanging from a rope attached to a long pole into the water, push down on the heavy weight on the other end of the pole and swing the pole over the field to empty the bucket.

STOP AT THE PYRAMIDS

It takes a few days to sail from Per-Ramessu to Thebes. When the boat reaches a place called Giza, you could spend a day or two here looking at the pyramids and temples. They are already over 1,000 years old at the time you are visiting.

Pyramids

Each pyramid was built for a pharaoh or queen to protect their bodies after death, so that their souls could enjoy the afterlife (see pages 22–23).

The Great Pyramid was built for Pharaoh Khufu around 2550 BCE. The other two pyramids were built for Pharaoh Khafre and Pharaoh Menkaure over the next 70 years, with smaller pyramids for their queens. For more than 4,000 years after it was built, the Great Pyramid was the tallest human-made structure in the world, standing 481 feet (146.6 m) tall.

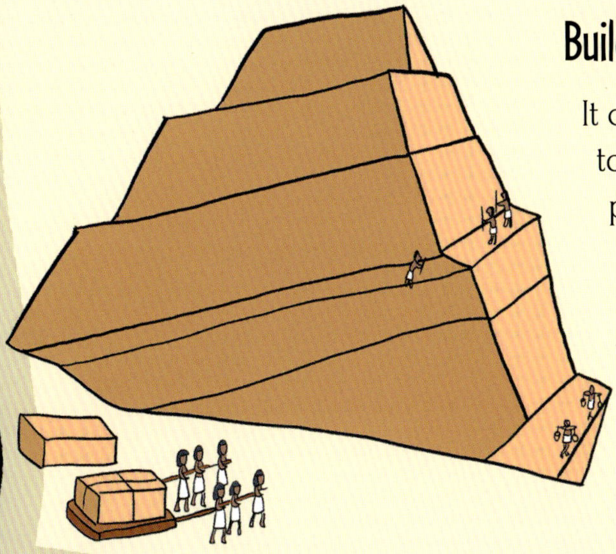

Building a pyramid

It could take 20 years and between 10,000 to 25,000 men to build a pyramid. Much of the limestone used to build pyramids was cut out of the ground from quarries nearby. Many historians believe that the blocks were pulled to the pyramid site on wooden sleds (and possibly up ramps made of wet sand) to where they were needed.

Stolen treasures

Despite the best efforts of pharaohs to protect their pyramid tombs with secret tunnels and sealed doorways, robbers broke in. They stole treasures – grave goods such as jewelry – and ruined the tombs. That's why pharaohs stopped building pyramids and instead started building rock tombs, such as those near Thebes in the Valley of the Kings (see pages 26–27).

Look out for: dangerous beasts

Hippos and crocodiles are both found near or in the Nile. Hippos have huge mouths and can capsize small boats. Crocodiles lurk in the reeds and will leap at the chance to eat you!

WHERE TO STAY

There are no inns or hotels in ancient Egypt, but luckily you have been invited to stay with a scribe you met on your journey to Thebes. A scribe is someone who reads and writes important documents. He leads you through the narrow streets, lined with mud-brick houses. He lives with his wife, seven children, his unmarried sisters, a guard dog, and two cats.

The scribe's home

Most people live in homes with several rooms, a courtyard at the back of the house, and steps up to a flat roof. Wealthy Egyptians have more and bigger rooms. Small windows keep the sun's heat out. In the scribe's courtyard, there is an outdoor oven where food is cooked. The scribe's young children often play on the roof.

Inside homes, travelers will notice a household altar in the first room. Every day the family brings gifts of food and drink to the small statues of gods and goddesses they worship there. The next room has a low seating area where people can sit in the day and sleep at night. There is another room where the family stores food.

Look out for: Taweret

Taweret is a household goddess who is believed to protect pregnant women and young children. She is part animal and part human with the body of a hippo, the legs of a lion, and the upper body and hair of a woman.

Top Tip

Prepare to share

Don't expect to be given a room of your own! It's normal for family members and guests to share a room.

Top Tip

Clean up

Ancient Egyptians like to keep clean. Ask for a bowl of water so that you can wash.

DRESS LIKE AN ANCIENT EGYPTIAN

Time travelers will find Thebes much easier to explore if they dress like ancient Egyptians, as their clothes help to keep them cool. Ask to borrow some clothes from the family you are staying with. Clothes are made from linen, a light fabric woven from threads of flax plants grown near the Nile.

Dress like an ancient Egyptian woman

An Egyptian woman usually wears a slim linen dress. Wealthy women's clothes are pleated to form folds. She'll add a cloak on top if it is cold. The richer you are, the finer the linen you can afford.

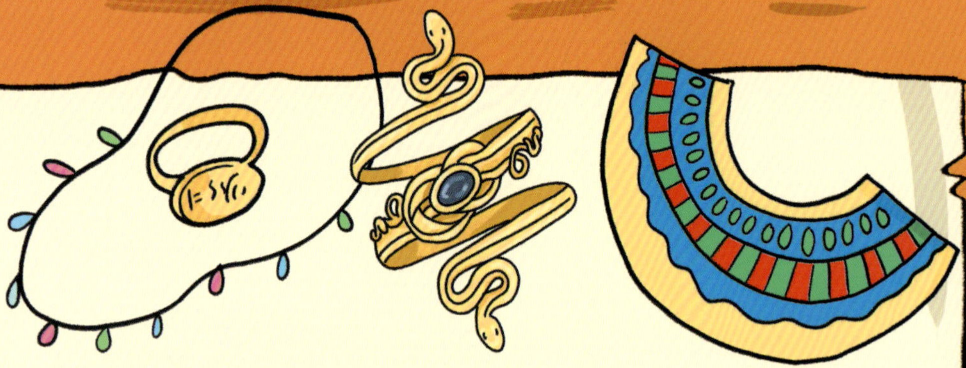

Look out for: jewelry

Travelers will notice that the Egyptians love jewelry – necklaces, bracelets, rings, and earrings. Wealthy people's jewelry is made from gold and precious stones, while poorer people have jewelry made from simple clay beads.

Dress like an ancient Egyptian man

Men often wear a "bag" tunic, tied at the waist with a linen sash, or a skirt tied at the waist. Men also wear cloaks in colder weather. Like other children, this man's son wears similar clothes to his father, just smaller. However, don't be shocked if you see younger children running around naked! This is quite normal in ancient Egypt.

Hair!

Men usually don't have beards or moustaches. Many people wear their hair short to stay cool in the heat and to try and avoid head lice. Wealthy people may shave their heads completely and wear wigs instead. You'll notice that children often have their heads shaved apart from one braid, called the sidelock of youth.

Sandals

On their feet, both men and women often wear sandals. They are woven from papyrus reeds into something that looks like a flip-flop. Wealthier people have leather sandals, but many people walk around barefoot.

Top Tip

Eye makeup

Everyone wears black eye makeup, so you'll need to learn how to do this. People think it protects their eyes from the strong Egyptian sunlight.

A GUIDE TO GODS AND GODDESSES

Time travelers will find this quick guide to some of the most important Egyptian gods and goddesses extremely useful. Ancient Egyptians believe that each god and goddess has influence over a certain part of daily life, the natural world or the afterlife. There are about 1,400 different gods and goddesses! Some are worshipped across the kingdom, while others are linked to local areas.

Amun-Ra (or Amun-Re)

Amun-Ra is king of the gods. Amun was the god of Thebes who then joined with Ra, the sun god, to become Amun-Ra. The temples at Karnak and Luxor in Thebes are dedicated to him (see pages 18–19).

Bastet

The cat goddess, Bastet, has the head of a cat and the body of a woman. People believe she keeps them safe from harm, protects homes, and brings good health and pleasure.

Anubis

Anubis is the god of mummification and the dead (see pages 22–25). He guides people on their journey to the afterlife. He is shown with the head of a jackal – a wild dog.

Hapi

People worship Hapi, god of the Nile, as he is said to bring the Nile floods every year (see page 8). He is usually shown as a man with blue skin and a round tummy.

Horus

An important god, Horus is shown with a hawk's head. He is the god of the sky and god of kingship, giving power to the pharaohs to rule on Earth.

Thoth

Thoth is the god of writing and knowledge, so he's special to scribes (see page 12). He has the head of an ibis bird. He acts as the scribe to the gods.

Seth

Ancient Egyptians fear Seth as he murdered his brother Osiris and is seen as the god of chaos. But they also admire him for his strength. He has the head of a mythical animal that looks a bit like the head of a greyhound dog.

Isis

The great mother goddess, Isis, has strong magical powers. She protects the king, protects the dead and brought her husband Osiris back to life.

Osiris

Osiris was brought back to life by Isis to become god of the afterlife. He is usually shown as a mummy with a white crown. His green face shows his link to new crops and farming.

VISIT SOME TEMPLES

It's time to get on with some sightseeing. Some must-see temples are found at Luxor and Karnak. Time travelers can reach them by foot, as they are in Thebes. An avenue of stone sphinxes, many with rams' heads, runs between the two temple sites.

Luxor and Karnak temples

The temples at Karnak and Luxor are dedicated to Amun-Ra, his wife Mut and their son, Khonsu. You can't miss the six enormous statues of Ramesses II at the entrance to Luxor Temple. He's not the first pharaoh to add to the temples, as they were built over several hundred years by different rulers.

Big and beautiful

The temples at Karnak are spread over a vast site. As well as shrines where statues of the gods and goddesses are worshipped, and towering gateways, there is a huge stone courtyard surrounded with pillars. There are also workshops where craftsmen make beautiful objects to be offered to the gods and goddesses.

Top Tip

Follow the rules

Near many temples you'll see a sacred lake where priests and priestesses bathe to make themselves clean enough to enter the temples. However hot you may be, don't be tempted to take a dip! It's strictly forbidden.

Look out for: priests and priestesses

Travelers aren't allowed inside most of the temple buildings. Only the royal family, priests, and priestesses can enter.

Inside temple shrines, priests and priestesses work hard to keep the gods and goddesses happy! They offer prayers, incense, gifts, and meals to statues, as they believe that the spirits of the gods and goddesses can live inside the statues. They also entertain the gods and goddesses with music and dancing.

Top Tip

Examine the walls

Take time to look at carved pictures on the outside of any temple you visit. These tell stories about gods, pharaohs, wars, and other events.

GO TO A FESTIVAL

While you are visiting Thebes, you may be able to enjoy a festival. There are over 60 festivals spread throughout the year. People join together to worship gods and goddesses, sing, dance, and feast.

Don't miss the statues

Festivals are one of the only times when ordinary people can get close to the statues of gods and goddesses kept inside temples. During the Beautiful Festival of the Valley, priests and priestesses carry the statues from the temples at Karnak across the Nile to visit temples on the other side. Musicians and dancers take part in the procession along streets lined with people cheering, dancing, and snacking on food given out as part of the festival. Over the river, the procession passes many tombs where people gather to share food at their relatives' burial places.

Feast time

Festivals are also a time for feasting at home. You have been invited to a banquet – a really grand meal – at a wealthy government advisor's home. His house is huge, with 30 rooms and a beautiful garden.

Servants offer guests drinks and fine food, while musicians and dancers provide the entertainment. Enjoy plates of fresh fruit and vegetables, as well as dishes with meat and fish. Most ancient Egyptians live on a diet of bread and beer, so take the chance to enjoy something different!

Top Tip

Dress up

Borrow some fine clothes and jewelry to attend the banquet. Wealthy Egyptians enjoy dressing up for festivals and feasts.

DEATH AND MUMMIFICATION

Ancient Egyptians love life and want it to go on forever after they die in a perfect version of life, called the afterlife. Since they believe that their soul will still need their human body in the afterlife, it needs to be mummified to preserve it. Ask an ancient Egyptian to describe how this is done. Only wealthier families can afford to mummify their relatives.

1. Soon after death, the family take the body of their dead relative across the Nile to the West Bank.

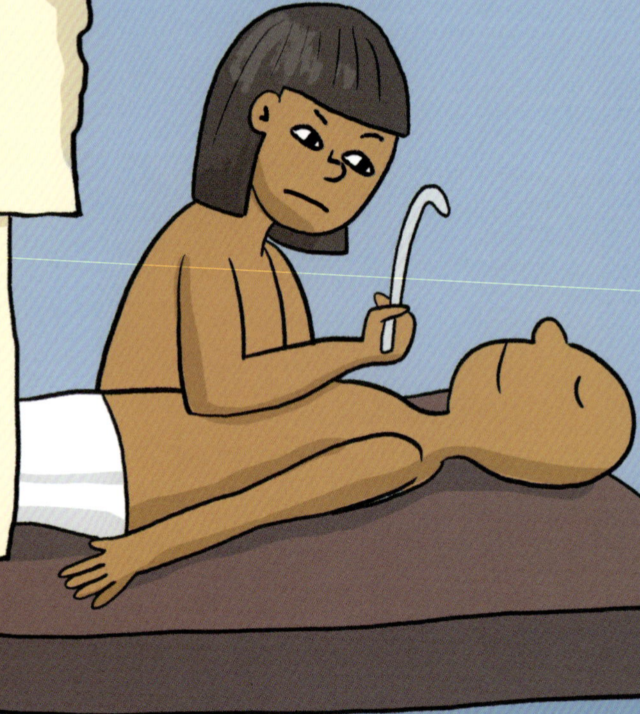

2. Here, special priests – called embalmers – wash the body. Using a metal hook, one man pulls the brain out through the nose and throws it away.

3. Now an embalmer makes a cut on the body using a knife made of a hard, black stone called obsidian. He removes most of the internal organs: the lungs, stomach, intestines, and liver. Each is placed in a canopic jar to be preserved separately.

4. The body is filled with a stuffing material (often straw), and covered with natron salt. Over 40 days, the natron salt dries out the body.

5. After removing the salt and the stuffing, embalmers pack the body with linen or sawdust. Then, the body is wrapped in up to 656 feet (200 m) of linen strips. This takes about two weeks.

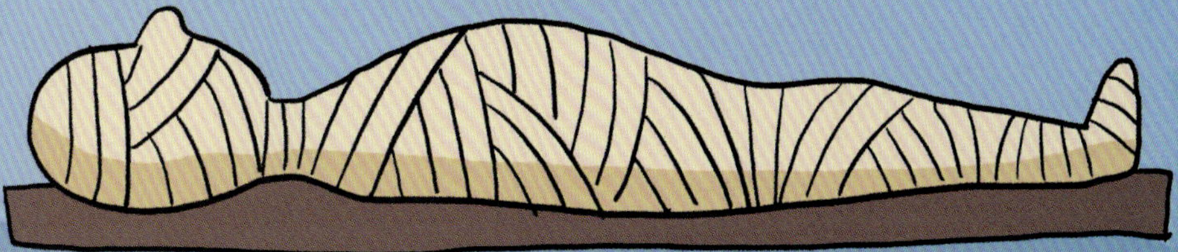

6. During the wrapping stage, small, beautiful objects called amulets are added to protect the body from evil or danger. The chief embalmer, wearing a mask of Anubis (see page 16), says prayers over the body.

Amulets

An amulet in the shape of a scarab beetle is often placed over the heart. A magic spell written on it is believed to protect the person in the afterlife. There were 143 amulets bound into the mummified body of the boy king, Tutankhamun, who was buried in the Valley of the Kings (see pages 26–27).

7. The mummy is covered by a linen cloth called a shroud and a metal or wooden mask is placed over the head. Now it is ready to be placed in a decorated coffin – called a sarcophagus – for burial. The whole process takes about 70 days.

WATCH A FUNERAL PROCESSION

Seventy days after someone dies, the family holds the funeral. You may see a funeral procession by crossing to the West Bank of the Nile. They are quite a sight to behold! Ancient Egyptians always bury their dead on that side of the river, either in simple graves or in underground rock-cut tombs, according to their wealth.

Walking to the tomb

At the front of a funeral procession for an important person, priests walk ahead of the coffin, leading the way to the tomb. Members of the family walk behind the coffin, beating their chests, pulling at their hair and throwing dust on their heads to show their grief. Wealthier families pay mourners to join the procession, singing sad songs, and weeping.

Behind them, servants carry things that will be buried in the tomb with the dead person. This includes the dead person's clothes, furniture, jewelry, makeup, and food and drink inside jars and pots – everything that the dead person might need in the afterlife.

Look out for: shabti servants

Egyptians want the afterlife to be perfect and that means they don't want to have to grow food, cook, clean, or do any work! It is grave goods – small figures called *shabtis* – that will do all these jobs for the dead person in the afterlife, acting as their servants.

Opening of the Mouth

Once the coffin reaches the tomb, the coffin is stood upright for the Opening of the Mouth ceremony. Priests – one wearing a mask of Anubis – and the dead person's sons recite spells. They use special tools to touch the mouth, eyes, ears, and nose on the face of the coffin. They believe this will make the dead person able to breathe, see, smell, and hear again in the afterlife.

Top Tip

Visit more temples

Don't forget to visit some more temples on this side of the river. These are the funerary temples, each built by a different pharaoh so their souls could be worshipped after their deaths. The funerary temple of the female pharaoh Hatshepsut is an impressive sight.

TUTANKHAMUN

By the time of Ramesses II, pharaohs are buried in secret rock-cut tombs in the Valley of the Kings. No one is allowed to visit them, to protect the tombs from robbers. Your scribe friend tells you what he's heard about the tomb of Pharaoh Tutankhamun, who died c. 1323 BCE. No one knows where his tomb is at the time of your visit, and it will stay that way until his tomb is discovered in 1922.

The boy king

When Tutankhamun became king in about 1332 BCE, he was about nine years old, so advisors helped him rule. About ten years later, aged around 19, he died. Like other pharaohs, he'd ordered the building of a rock-cut tomb to be buried in, but he died before it was finished. Tutankhamun was buried in another small tomb that had been built earlier for another purpose, but not used.

Tomb robbers

Even though the tomb locations are secret, ancient Egyptian tomb robbers will still find and rob most of the tombs in the Valley of the Kings. Tutankhamun's tomb, however, was never discovered by tomb robbers.

Tomb for Tut

Steep stairs lead down from the entrance to four rooms in his small tomb. The burial chamber is decorated with wall paintings, including scenes showing Tutankhamun in the afterlife. This is where the pharaoh's mummified body lies inside three coffins, which have in turn been placed inside a sarcophagus (stone coffin). Other rooms are full of over 5,000 treasures that are thought to be useful to Tutankhamun in the afterlife.

TOP TIP

Visit the workers' village

All the work on tombs and temples needs a huge number of skilled workers, such as craftsmen, builders, and wall painters. Ask to be taken to visit the village where workers live with their families. It's called Deir el-Medina.

VISIT QUICK!

Pharaoh Ramesses II will live to an old age, ruling for 66 years. At this time, Egypt's power and wealth is declining, but it is still a great time to visit.

A divided country

About 300 years after Ramesses II's death, around the year 1000 BCE, Egypt became a divided country. Priests ruled the south of the country from Thebes, and pharaohs continued to rule the north. Over time, foreign invaders attacked Egypt and eventually succeeded in placing themselves in power.

Cleopatra VII was the last pharaoh to rule Egypt. Cleopatra was born in Egypt, but her ancestors were actually Macedonian Greek. Finally, in 30 BCE, Egypt became part of the Roman Empire.

Cleopatra VII

How do we know about the ancient Egyptians?

Luckily for us, a huge number of objects, statues, buildings, and mummified bodies survive from the time of the ancient Egyptians. Egypt's hot, dry weather helped preserve buildings and statues. Tombs packed with grave goods and decorated with carvings and wall paintings help historians work out the beliefs and way of life of ancient Egyptian people.

Helpful hieroglyphs

One of the main reasons we know so much about the ancient Egyptians is because they invented a writing system using picture signs called hieroglyphs. Scribes used these to keep records and write notes.

Craftsmen carved hieroglyphs onto the walls of temples, tombs and statues, recording stories of the gods, pharaohs or important people.

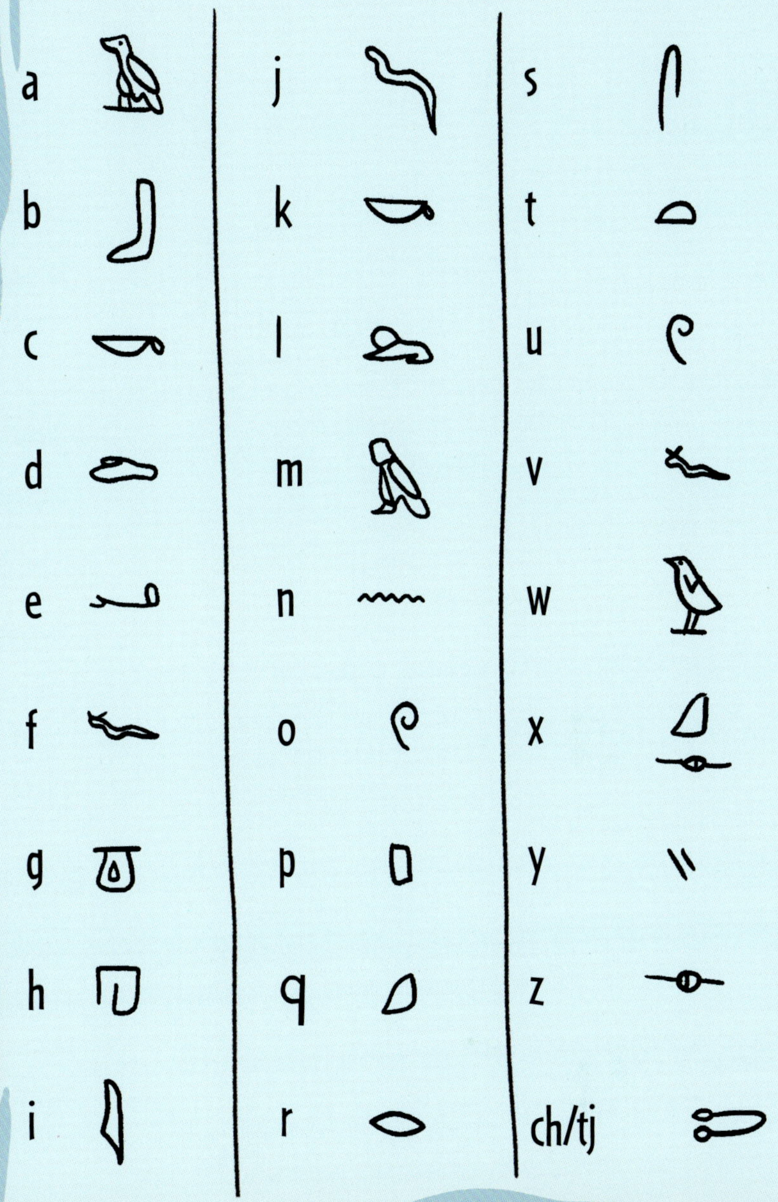

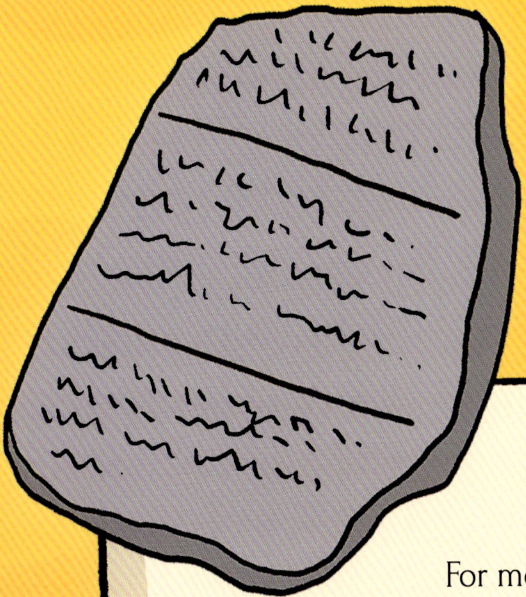

The Rosetta Stone

For more than 1,000 years after the end of the ancient Egyptian civilization, no one knew how to read hieroglyphs. After the discovery of the Rosetta Stone in 1799, people gradually figured out how to read them. The Rosetta Stone has the same message carved in it, in three different types of writing. One of them is ancient Greek, which scholars can read. By 1822, this helped them to finally succeed in unlocking the mystery of ancient Egyptian writing.

Time travelers can use this simple alphabet (above) to start learning how to read and write ancient Egyptian hieroglyphs for themselves.

GLOSSARY

Afterlife Life after death.

Altar A flat stone or table used for religious worship.

Amulet A piece of jewelry or a small decorative object, carried by an ancient Egyptian, or placed on a mummy, as protection from evil.

Archaeologist Someone who studies history by examining objects, buildings, and ruins from the past.

Ceremony An event that celebrates or marks something, such as an achievement, death, or religious event.

Chaos Confusion and disorder.

Delta A low-lying area of land where a river splits into smaller rivers to empty into a large body of water, such as a sea or a lake.

Dynasty A series of rulers that belong to the same family.

Embalmer Someone who knows how to preserve a dead body, making it ready for burial and slowing down the process of decay.

Flax A plant grown for the fibers in its stem, which can be made into linen cloth.

Incense Strong, scented smoke made by burning certain woods or oils.

Limestone A sedimentary rock.

Merchant Someone who buys and sells goods, often transporting them to markets.

Natron salt A salt found in lake beds.

Obelisk A tall, pointed stone pillar.

Ox A male cow. (Plural: oxen.)

Papyrus A paper-like material made from the stems of water plants.

Plow A farm tool used to break up or turn over soil, ready for planting.

Quarry A place where people dig stone, sand, or other materials out of the ground.

Roman Empire A large empire that centerd on Rome and spread through much of Europe and the Mediterranean region, between the 8th century BCE and 476 CE.

Sacred Something that is considered important to religious people.

Sarcophagus A stone coffin.

Soul The spiritual part of someone. Many people believe it lives on after death.

Sphinx A stone figure with a lion's body and the head of a human or animal.

FURTHER INFORMATION

Books

A History of Africa: From Prehistory to Today
Robin Walker (Franklin Watts, 2024)

A Question of History: What Happened to the Pharaoh's Brain?
Tim Cooke (Wayland, 2021)

Uncover History: Ancient Egypt
Rachel Minay (Wayland, 2023)

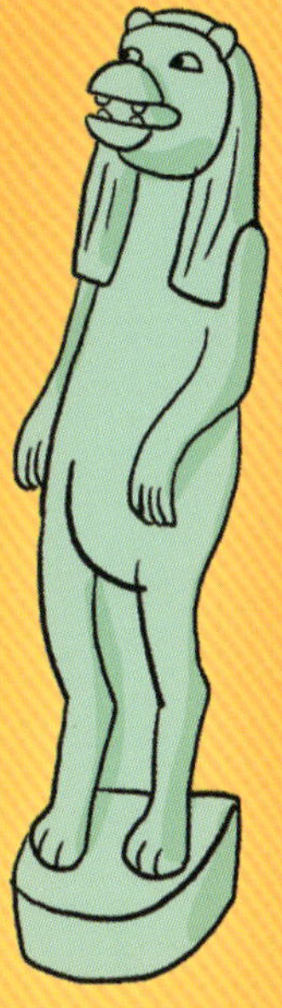

Websites

Discover more ancient Egyptian facts and information at:
https://kids.nationalgeographic.com/history/article/ancient-egypt

For lots of facts on the ancient Egyptians, visit this BBC Bitesize website:
www.bbc.co.uk/bitesize/topics/zg87xnb

Find more information about the ancient Egyptians at this Britannica Kids website:
https://kids.britannica.com/kids/article/ancient-Egypt/353087

INDEX